GRANDPA AND LUCY

A Story about Love
and Dementia

by Edie Weinstein

To Kiera and Connor;

Grandparents can be <u>wonderful</u> friends!
Enjoy your time with Grandma Lolo
and Grandma Sue and cherish the
memories! Keep connecting!

—Edie Weinstein

ILLUSTRATIONS BY

Claire Aamodt • Adeleine Cooper • Will Hoppe
Ela Paske • Caroline Weier • Edie Weinstein • Shane Zenk

Inky Puppy Paws • Saint Paul, Minnesota • 2017

D1362289

Text copyright © 2017 by Edie Weinstein
Illustrations copyright © 2017 by Claire Aamodt, Adeleine Cooper, Will Hoppe,
    Ela Paske, Caroline Weier, Edie Weinstein, and Shane Zenk

Typesetting/Layout Design by Kristin Smith
Content Review and Production Coordination provided by ACT on Alzheimer's

ISBN: 978-1-9782-8882-9
Library of Congress Control Number: 2017916107
CreateSpace Independent Publishing Platform, North Charleston, SC

For inquiries, contact Inky Puppy Paws: inkypuppypaws@gmail.com

Manufactured in the United States of America
10 9 8 7 6 5 4 3 2 1

ACKNOWLEDGMENTS

The author thanks her parents and family for supporting the Girl Scouts and this Girl Scout Silver Award Project, as well as Meghan Constantini and everyone at St. Paul Neighborhoods ACT on Alzheimer's for teaching her about dementia, providing support, and helping her achieve this goal.

Thanks to Ethical Leaders in Action for donating to the cause and to Davanni's Pizza for lending to us its back room to work on this project all summer. Last but not least, thanks to the team of illustrators who helped make this book a reality. You've given so much time and effort to make this book beautiful.

Together as illustrators, friends, and graduates of Nativity of Our Lord School, St. Paul, MN. *Left to right:* Ela Paske, Edie Weinstein, Will Hoppe, Shane Zenk, Caroline Weier, Adeleine Cooper, and Claire Aamodt.

To everyone in the world who is
affected by dementia

Lucy snatched her hat off the hook and pulled the door shut behind her. The birds chirped, and the sun was bright in the fresh air.

"Lucy, hurry or we'll be late to see Grandpa!" Lucy's mother called from the car.

"I'm coming!" Lucy answered and skipped to the car.

When they got to Grandpa's house, Lucy bounded out of the car and up to the front door. She rapped on the wood and bobbed up and down, excited to see her beloved grandpa.

Grandpa flung open the door and wrapped Lucy in a warm hug.

"Hey, sweetie! How are you?" he cried.
"Awesome!" Lucy said happily. "What are we going to do today?"

"Well," whispered Grandpa, getting down on one knee, "I thought we would go to the movie *Princess Butterfly*."
"Hooray! I love princess movies!" Lucy shouted.

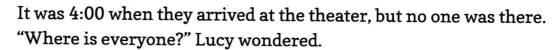

It was 4:00 when they arrived at the theater, but no one was there. "Where is everyone?" Lucy wondered.

"I bet they're coming. I remember that the movie starts at 4:45. I know it," said Grandpa.

Mom raised her eyebrows. "Are you sure? Let me see the tickets."

Grandpa looked through all his pockets but found nothing. Lucy hung her head in disappointment.

"Huh, I must have misplaced them. No big deal. We can walk home to get the tickets and still make it in time for the movie."

Lucy and her mother looked through the entire house before they found the theater tickets, crumpled under the couch.

"But, Grandpa, these tickets say the movie was yesterday at 2:30," Lucy muttered.

Grandpa turned to face Lucy. "No, Miranda. I know those tickets are for today at 4:00."

"My name is Lucy," she said.

Grandpa's face turned red. "Don't you think I know your name?" he yelled. Lucy shrank back in fear. "Now just because I lost some silly tickets and got a number confused doesn't mean you can be disrespectful!"

Lucy was speechless. Grandpa had never, ever shouted at her before. She sniffed and wiped her eyes.

Lucy and Mom left quickly. As soon as she got in the car, Lucy burst into tears.

When they got home, Lucy crawled onto her mother's lap.
"Why would Grandpa yell at me like that?" she asked her mother, who sighed.
"Sweetie, we need to talk," Mom said.

"Your grandpa has a kind of dementia called Alzheimer's disease. It's when certain parts of the brain stop remembering things like it's supposed to," she explained.

"Then why did Grandpa yell at me?" Lucy was still confused.

"He might be embarrassed that he forgot when the movie was, which could make him angry," Mom said.

"Well, how did he forget? He still remembers all of his old army stories. He told me one in the car," Lucy reminded her mother.

"Think of it this way. Grandpa's brain is like a bookshelf. All the old memories, like his army memories and his childhood memories, are at the bottom, and the new ones, like what time the movie is or what he had for breakfast today, are at the top. If someone big and strong shakes the bookshelf, which ones will fall—the ones at the top or the ones at the bottom?"

"The top ones!" Lucy exclaimed.

"Exactly," Mom nodded. "So that's why he can tell you a story about the army in 1970 but not what time we were supposed to be at the movie today. The army stories are the books that stick on the bottom shelf that are older and more stable, but the movie time is the book at the top that falls first."

The day's earlier events were beginning to make sense to Lucy, though something was still bothering her.

"But, Mom, why did he call me Miranda? That's your name! It hurt my feelings. Doesn't he love me enough to know my name?"

"Lucy, of course he loves you! He just can't remember little things like names or times," Mom said with a smile. "It's also very important that you try not to tell Grandpa he's wrong. If he says something that's not true, just smile and be respectful. And if he calls you Miranda, just move on in the conversation. Ask him for another army story if you like."

The next day, Lucy went back to visit Grandpa. She nervously walked up to the door but hesitated before she knocked. Glancing back one more time at her smiling mother, she finally banged on the door.

Once again the door flew open, and Lucy found herself lifted into the air by Grandpa's hug.

"How's my sweet pea, Miranda?" Grandpa asked, ruffling her hair.

Lucy took a deep breath and said, "I brought fun things to do today!"

Mom handed her a bag of activities to show Grandpa.

Going into the living room, Lucy pulled out an old photo album and remembered what her mother had told her: "A good activity is to show him photographs of his childhood. They will spark memories that you two can talk about."

She flipped to a black and white picture of a house, and Grandpa smiled.

"That was my aunt's house! On her mantle was a jar that was full of blue sweets . . ." Grandpa told Lucy all about his aunt.

Lucy listened to his story with a smile.

After looking at many photos and listening to the funny stories that went with each one, Lucy pulled the next activity from her bag—a CD player and a CD that Mom had helped her to make.

She pressed PLAY, and Frank Sinatra's music began to waft through the living room. Right away, Grandpa stood up and started dancing with Lucy. She giggled as he swung her around the living room.

She thought back to what her mother had said: "Music he knew will spark some more stories. Just play him some Frank Sinatra!"

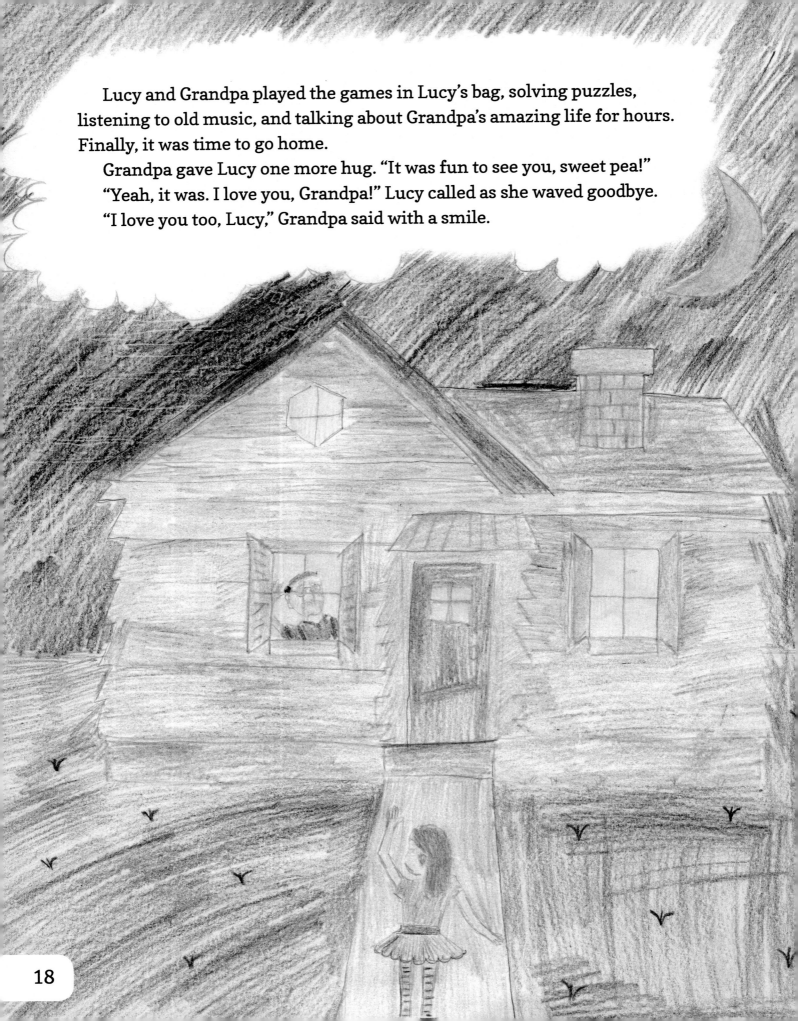

Lucy and Grandpa played the games in Lucy's bag, solving puzzles, listening to old music, and talking about Grandpa's amazing life for hours. Finally, it was time to go home.

Grandpa gave Lucy one more hug. "It was fun to see you, sweet pea!"

"Yeah, it was. I love you, Grandpa!" Lucy called as she waved goodbye.

"I love you too, Lucy," Grandpa said with a smile.

Afterword

Lots of girls and boys have a family member or a friend who has dementia like Lucy's grandpa. Alzheimer's disease is one type of dementia that affects a person's brain and makes it harder to recall recent memories. Dementia may also cause persons to repeat themselves or to act in ways different from before. It may feel strange when friends or family members forget something or act differently, but there are still many ways for everyone around to connect with them.

Lucy used several ways to connect with Grandpa and to learn more about him. By looking at old photographs or listening to old music, you can hear stories and better get to know an older family member or friend. Doing puzzles is also fun, along with reading books or going for walks. If persons with dementia say something that's not true, it's better to change the subject or agree with them than to tell them they are wrong. Persons with dementia don't always remember they have a memory problem, so it might hurt their feelings if you correct them. Sometimes dementia can change the way persons act or feel and arguing with them is not helpful; it can hurt their feelings and make things worse.

The most important thing while interacting with persons with dementia is to do your best to be kind and to keep spending time with them. You'll probably learn something you didn't know about them! Lots of grandparents have cool stories you may not have heard before.

Above all, enjoy your time with your loved one and keep learning about the world around you.

Five Key Messages

- Dementia is not a normal part of aging.
- Dementia is caused by diseases of the brain.
- Dementia is not just about having memory problems.
- It is possible to have a good quality of life with dementia.
- There's more to a person than the dementia.

Source

The information about dementia in this book, including the bookcase story, was adapted from a Dementia Friends Information Session. Dementia Friends is a global movement that is changing the way people think, act, and talk about dementia. The program was originally developed by the Alzheimer's Society in the United Kingdom. Dementia Friends Minnesota is an initiative of ACT on Alzheimer's.

Learn more at www.ACTonALZ.org.

Giving Back

A portion of the proceeds from the sale of this book will be used to support Alzheimer's education and outreach.

Made in the USA
Lexington, KY
25 November 2017